VIETNAMESE COOKBOOK

MAIN COURSE – 80+ Quick and easy to prepare at home recipes, step-by-step guide to the classic Vietnamese cuisine

TABLE OF CONTENTS

BREAKFAST 7

FRIED RICE 7

ASPARAGUS AND CRAB SOUP 8

RICE SOUP WITH CHICKEN 9

PRESSED RICE LONGS 11

GRILLED PORK WITH RICE NOODLES 12

RICE SOUP WITH FISH & GINGER 13

CHICKEN RICE SOUP 14

BEEF RICE SOUP AND GINGER 16

VIETNAMESE RICE SOUP 17

COCONUT CASSAVA CAKE 18

CELLOPHONE NOODLE SOUP 19

RICE SOUP 20

VIETNAMESE ICED COFFE 21

CRISPY DUMPLINGS 22

VIETNAMESE BAGUETTE 23

SAUSAGE AND SALTED DUCK EGG CUPCAKE 24

BAKED SHRIMP TOATS 26

RICE NOODLES WITH BEEF AND BOK CHOY 27

VIETNAMESE CROISSANTS 28

VIETNAMESE COOKIES 29

LUNCH 32

FISH SOUP 32

CHICKEN BAGUETTES 33

LAMB SHANKS WITH SWEET POTATOES 35

CHICKEN SALAD	36
PEPPER SQUID	37
VEGGIE HOTPOT	39
SALMON NOODLE SOUP	40
SEAFOOD SALAD	41
PRAWN SUMMER ROLLS	42
CARAMEL TROUT	44
PRAWN SALAD	45
VIETNAMESE SALAD	46
ASIAN CABBAGE & PRAWN SALAD	47
ASIAN CHICKEN SALAD	49
CARROT, RED CABBAGE & ONION SALAD	50
PINEAPPLE SALAD	51
NOODLE SALAD	52
PRAWN NOODLE SALAD	53
ASIAN NOODLE & TURKEY SOUP	55
TOFU & CASHEW STIR-FRY	56
DINNER	59
LEMONGRASS CHICKEN	59
BEAN CURD SHIK WITH SHRIMP	60
CHICKEN CURRY	61
SUMMER ROLLS	63
CRAB WITH CHILI	64
CRAB NOODLES	66
GARLIC NOODLES	67
LEMONGRASS BEEF SKEWERS	68

- SRIRACHA GRILLED SHRIMP 70
- POK POK WINGS 71
- BANH MI WIH LEMONGRASS PORK 72
- LEMONGRASS SHRIMP 74
- SPRING ROLLS 75
- CARAMEL SHRIMP 76
- GRILLED SHRIMP WITH GREEN PAPAYA 77
- CARAMEL CHICKEN 79
- SUGAR CANE SHRIMP 80
- CHICKEN WINGS 81
- LEMONGRASS WINGS 82
- GRILLED CHICKEN BANH MI 84
- DESSERT 86
- SINH TO – FRUIT SHAKE 86
- VIETNAMESE EGG ROLLS 87
- COFFE CRÈME FLAN 88
- STICKY RICE WITH COCONUT 89
- FRIEND SPRING ROLLS 90
- PAPAYA MIX 91
- SUGAR CANE JUICE 92
- VIETNAMESE BROWNIE 93
- VIETNAMESE COFFE FLAN 95
- VIETNAMESE ICED COFFE 96
- VIETNAMESE AVOCADO SMOOTHIE 97
- VIETNAMESE EGG SODA 98
- VIETNAMESE COFFEE POPS 99

VIETNAMESE EGG COFFEE	100
VIETNAMESE YOGURT	101
VIETNAMESE COFFEE FRAPPE	102
COCONUT MILK COFFEE	103
CHERRY SMOOTHIE	104
VIETNAMESE GRANITA	105
VIETNAMESE GREEN SMOOTHIE	106

☞Copyright 2018 by Noah Jerris - All rights reserved.

This document is geared towards providing exact and reliable information in regards to the topic and issue covered. The publication is sold with the idea that the publisher is not required to render accounting, officially permitted, or otherwise, qualified services. If advice is necessary, legal or professional, a practiced individual in the profession should be ordered.

- From a Declaration of Principles which was accepted and approved equally by a Committee of the American Bar Association and a Committee of Publishers and Associations.

In no way is it legal to reproduce, duplicate, or transmit any part of this document in either electronic means or in printed format. Recording of this publication is strictly prohibited and any storage of this document is not allowed unless with written permission from the publisher. All rights reserved.

The information provided herein is stated to be truthful and consistent, in that any liability, in terms of inattention or otherwise, by any usage or abuse of any policies, processes, or directions contained within is the solitary and utter responsibility of the recipient reader. Under no circumstances will any legal responsibility or blame be held against the publisher for any reparation, damages, or monetary loss due to the information herein, either directly or indirectly.

Respective authors own all copyrights not held by the publisher.

The information herein is offered for informational purposes solely, and is universal as so. The presentation of the information is without contract or any type of guarantee assurance.

The trademarks that are used are without any consent, and the publication of the trademark is without permission or backing by the trademark owner. All trademarks and brands within this book are for clarifying purposes only and are the owned by the owners themselves, not affiliated with this document.

Introduction

Vietnamese recipes for personal enjoyment but also for family enjoyment. You will love them for sure for how easy it is to prepare them.

BREAKFAST

FRIED RICE

Serves: **4**

Prep Time: **10**   Minutes

Cook Time: **20**   Minutes

Total Time: **30**   Minutes

INGREDIENTS

- ½ cup canola oil
- 5-ounces shrimp
- 3 cups white rice
- ½ tsp salt
- ½ tsp sugar
- ¼ tsp pepper
- 2 eggs
- 2 cups leafy greens
- 2 tsp seasoning sauce
- 2 tsp fish sauce
- ¾ cup sliced scallions

DIRECTIONS

1. In a wok add oil over medium heat, add shrimp and cook for 2-3 minutes, when ready transfer the shrimp to bowl and set aside
2. In another bowl stir in black pepper, rice, salt, sugar and mix well
3. Into a pan crack the eggs, add rice and toss to combine
4. Add greens, shrimp and toss to mix well
5. Add fish sauce, seasoning sauce and mix well
6. Remove from heat and stir in scallion before serving

ASPARAGUS AND CRAB SOUP

Serves: **4**

Prep Time: **15** Minutes

Cook Time: **30** Minutes

Total Time: **45** Minutes

INGREDIENTS

- 5 cups chicken stock
- salt
- 2 tablespoons cornstarch
- 1/3 lbs. crabmeat
- ½ tsp fish sauce

- ¼ tsp black pepper
- 1 egg
- ¾ lbs. asparagus
- 1 tablespoon canola oil
- 1 shallot

DIRECTIONS

1. In a saucepan bring the stock to boil, add asparagus cook for 10-15 minutes, remove from heat, set aside to allow the asparagus flavor to develop
2. In a saucepan heat oil over medium heat, add shallot and cook for 4-5 minutes, add the crabmeat and cook for another 2-3 minutes, add pepper, fish sauce and salt
3. Bring the soup to a simmer, add the crab mixture and taste
4. Turn off the heat, pour the beaten egg and stir gently
5. Serve when ready

RICE SOUP WITH CHICKEN

Serves: 6
Prep Time: 20 Minutes
Cook Time: 30 Minutes

Total Time: **50** Minutes

INGREDIENTS

- 1 boneless chicken breast
- 2 tablespoons canola oil
- salt
- ½ lbs. shrimp
- ½ cup tapioca pears
- ½ cup scallion
- ½ cup cilantro
- 1 cup white rice
- 2-quarts chicken stock
- 4 dried ear mushrooms
- ½ cup crabmeat
- 1 onion

DIRECTIONS

1. In a saucepan add water and chicken broth and bring to boil
2. Return water to boil and add rice, cook for 5-10 minutes
3. Bring stock to boil, add mushrooms, chicken rice and lower the heat for 10-12 minutes
4. In a skillet cook onion for 4-5 minutes, add shrimp, crabmeat and stir
5. Add the tapioca pearls and cook for 10-12 minutes, shrimp mixture and adjust with salt

6. Remove from heat sprinkle with the scallion and serve

PRESSED RICE LONGS

Serves: **4**

Prep Time: **30** Minutes

Cook Time: **10** Minutes

Total Time: **40** Minutes

INGREDIENTS

- 2 cups rice

DIRECTIONS

1. Cook the rice until soft, add extra water if necessary
2. Fluff the rice and place half of it on a towel
3. Gather up the tower
4. When the rice is compact open up the towel and shape the rice into a log, put the log on a plate
5. Allow the logs to cool until they are dry and serve

GRILLED PORK WITH RICE NOODLES

Serves: **4**

Prep Time: **20** Minutes

Cook Time: **30** Minutes

Total Time: **50** Minutes

INGREDIENTS

- Vegetable garnish plate

MARINADE

- 1 shallot
- 2 lbs. pork
- 2/3 lbs. rice noodles
- 1 cup dipping sauce
- 2 tsp sugar
- ¾ tsp black pepper
- 1 tablespoon caramel sauce
- 2 tablespoons fish sauce
- 2 tablespoons canola oil

DIRECTIONS

1. In a bowl mix sugar, pepper, shallot and transfer mixture to a bowl with caramel sauce, oil and fish sauce
2. Add pork and refrigerate for 3-4 hours
3. Add the noodles on 2-3 plates and set aside with the dipping sauce and vegetables
4. Grill the pork for 4-5 minutes per side, transfer to a plate and serve

RICE SOUP WITH FISH & GINGER

Serves: **4**

Prep Time: **10** Minutes

Cook Time: **30** Minutes

Total Time: **40** Minutes

INGREDIENTS

- 1 red onion
- 2/4 lbs. white fish

MARINADE

- ½ tsp salt
- 1 scallion
- ½ tsp sugar

- 1 tablespoon canola oil
- 1 tablespoon fish sauce
- 2 tablespoons cider vinegar
- 2 tablespoons ginger
- 2 tablespoons cilantro
- 6 cups rice

DIRECTIONS

1. In a bowl mix the following marinade ingredients: ginger, cilantro, salt, sugar, fish sauce, oil and add fish and onion, set aside
2. In a saucepan, bring to boil the rice soup, divide the fish among the soup bowls
3. Garnish with scallion and serve

CHICKEN RICE SOUP

Serves: 4
Prep Time: 40 Minutes
Cook Time: 20 Minutes
Total Time: 60 Minutes

INGREDIENTS

- ¼ lbs. boneless chicken
- 1 tablespoon fish sauce
- 1 tablespoon canola oil
- 1 onion
- 6 cups rice soup
- salt
- 1 tablespoon cilantro leaves
- 1 scallion

DIRECTIONS

1. In a bowl toss the chicken with the fish sauce and set aside
2. In a skillet add onion, cook for 4-5 minutes, add the chicken and sauté for 4-5 minutes
3. Add the chicken mixture to the saucepan holding the rice soup
4. Bring to boil, add salt if necessary
5. Top with scallion and serve

BEEF RICE SOUP AND GINGER

Serves: **4**

Prep Time: **10** Minutes

Cook Time: **30** Minutes

Total Time: **40** Minutes

INGREDIENTS

- 2 tablespoons cilantro leaves
- 1 scallion
- black pepper
- salt
- ½ lbs. beef steak
- 1 tablespoon fresh ginger

DIRECTIONS

1. To each soup bowl add beef, scattering it in small pieces, add salt and ginger
2. In a saucepan bring rice to boil, ladle it over the beef and garnish with scallion, pepper and serve

VIETNAMESE RICE SOUP

Serves: *4*
Prep Time: 10   Minutes

Cook Time: 20   Minutes

Total Time: 30   Minutes

INGREDIENTS

- ¾ cup rice
- 1 scallion
- salt
- 2-quarts chicken stock
- 4 quarter-sized slices ginger

DIRECTIONS

1. In a saucepan add rice, water and cover
2. Add ginger, scallion, stock and boil over low heat
3. Let the soup cook for 5-10 minutes, cover and cook for another hour
4. Remove from heat, add salt and serve

COCONUT CASSAVA CAKE

Serves: **6**

Prep Time: **10** Minutes

Cook Time: **30** Minutes

Total Time: **40** Minutes

INGREDIENTS

- 1 package grated cassava
- 1 cup coconut milk
- 1 egg
- 1 cup mung bean
- 1 cup sugar
- 2 tablespoons cornstarch
- ½ cup water

DIRECTIONS

1. In a bowl stir in cornstarch and sugar
2. In another bowl whisk together coconut milk, egg and water
3. Add wet ingredients to dry ingredients and mix well
4. Add cassava, mung bean and whisk well
5. Bake for 1 hours at 375 F or until golden brown

6. Remove cut into wedges and serve

CELLOPHONE NOODLE SOUP

Serves: 6

Prep Time: 20 Minutes

Cook Time: 30 Minutes

Total Time: 50 Minutes

INGREDIENTS

- 3-quarts chicken stock
- 2 tablespoons fish sauce
- sugar
- salt
- 3 dried wood ear mushrooms
- ½ lbs. cellophane noodles
- black pepper
- ¾ lbs. boneless chicken breast

DIRECTIONS

1. In a pot bring stock to boil, add chicken breast and cook for a couple of minutes, remove from pot

2. Add sugar and fish sauce to stock and bring to boil
3. Add noodles, mushrooms, chicken and boil
4. Transfer to soup bowls garnish with coriander or pepper and serve

RICE SOUP

Serves: **4**

Prep Time: **20** Minutes

Cook Time: **10** Minutes

Total Time: **30** Minutes

INGREDIENTS

- ¾ cup rice
- 2 scallions
- salt
- 2-quarts chicken stock
- 4 slices fresh ginger

DIRECTIONS

1. In a saucepan add rice and cover with water
2. Add ginger, scallion, stock and bring to boil

3. Lower the heat and simmer for 5-10 minutes
4. Cover and cook for one hour
5. Taste and add salt if necessary before serving

VIETNAMESE ICED COFFE

Serves: *1*

Prep Time: *10* Minutes

Cook Time: *20* Minutes

Total Time: *30* Minutes

INGREDIENTS

- 2 tablespoons dark ground coffee
- 2 tablespoons condensed milk

DIRECTIONS

1. Steep coffee grounds in a heatproof container with boiling water for 4-5 minutes
2. Pour through ha coffee filter into a heatproof glass and serve

CRISPY DUMPLINGS

Serves: **6**

Prep Time: **30** Minutes

Cook Time: **30** Minutes

Total Time: **60** Minutes

INGREDIENTS

- ¾ lbs. gyoza skin
- ½ tsp salt
- 5 oz. water
- 2/4 lbs. all-purpose flour
- 1 tsp baking powder
- 1 tsp sugar

FILLING

- 1 lb. pork
- ½ cup carrot
- salt, sugar, pepper, stock powder
- 2 oz. glass noodle
- 0.5 oz. mushroom
- 2 tablespoons shallot

DIRECTIONS

1. In a bowl mix baking powder, salt, sugar, flour, water and mix well
2. Season the pork with pepper, sugar, salt and stock powder
3. Mix with shallot, glass noodle, carrot and mushroom and set aside
4. Place a spoonful of the filling in the center of the wrapper
5. In a saucepan heat cooking oil, deep-fry the dumplings till golden brown, serve with greens and dipping fish sauce

VIETNAMESE BAGUETTE

Serves: *1*
Prep Time: *10* Minutes
Cook Time: *20* Minutes
Total Time: *30* Minutes

INGREDIENTS

- 1 baguette roll
- mayonnaise
- maggi seasoning sauce

- liver pâte
- 3 cucumber strips
- 2 springs cilantro
- 3 slices jalapeno
- ½ cup carrot pickle

DIRECTIONS

1. Slit the bread lengthwise and preheat toaster to 300 F
2. Spread the mayonnaise over the bread and drizzle with seasoning sauce
3. Layer the meat, cilantro chile, pickle, cucumber
4. Serve when ready

SAUSAGE AND SALTED DUCK EGG CUPCAKE

Serves: 4
Prep Time: 20 Minutes
Cook Time: 30 Minutes
Total Time: 50 Minutes

INGREDIENTS

- 1 cup self-rising flour
- 1 cup butter
- 1 cup sugar
- 3 large eggs
- ¾ cup milk
- ½ cup orange juice
- 2 tsp orange zest
- 5 salted eggs
- cilantro
- 1 cup all-purpose flour

DIRECTIONS

1. In a bowl mix self rising flour and all purpose flour
2. In a bowl mix with an electric mixer
3. Add sugar, eggs and flour mixture, orange juice and blend
4. Add in the zest to the batter and mix well
5. Spoon the batter into the cupcakes liners, garnish with cilantro
6. Bake for 20 minutes at 350 F, remove and serve

BAKED SHRIMP TOATS

Serves: **8**

Prep Time: **20** Minutes

Cook Time: **30** Minutes

Total Time: **50** Minutes

INGREDIENTS

- 10 slices white bread
- 1 tablespoon canola oil
- ¼ tsp black pepper
- 1 clove garlic
- 1 egg
- 2 tablespoon minced scallion
- 2 tablespoon butter
- ½ tsp water
- 1 lb. shrimp
- salt
- 1 tsp cornstarch
- ½ tsp sugar

DIRECTIONS

1. Preheat oven to 275, bake the bread sliced for 25 minutes
2. In a bowl mix shrimp with slat, sugar, pepper, garlic, cornstarch, egg white, oil and mix well
3. Transfer to a blender and blend until smooth
4. The paste should be thick
5. Spread the mixture on bread, bake for 5-6 minutes and serve

RICE NOODLES WITH BEEF AND BOK CHOY

Serves: 4

Prep Time: 20 Minutes

Cook Time: 30 Minutes

Total Time: 50 Minutes

INGREDIENTS

- 10 oz. rice noodles
- 5 oz beef flank steak
- 2 tablespoons canola oil
- 2 tsp fish sauce
- 2 tsp soy sauce

- ½ tsp cornstarch
- ½ tsp salt
- 2 cups bok choy
- 1 cup mung bean sprouts

DIRECTIONS

1. In a bowl mix beef with oil, soy sauce, fish sauce and cornstarch
2. In a wok add water, oil, beef and stir-fry, cook for 5-6 minutes and transfer the meat to a plate
3. Add noodles and bok choy and fry for 1-2 minutes, add bean sprouts, fish soy sauce and toss well
4. Return the cooked beef cook for another 1-2 minutes
5. Transfer to a plate and serve

VIETNAMESE CROISSANTS

Serves: **8**

Prep Time: **10** Minutes

Cook Time: **20** Minutes

Total Time: **30** Minutes

INGREDIENTS

- 1 ball croissant dough
- 1 egg white
- 1 tablespoon water
- salt
- 1 can chocolate chips

DIRECTIONS

1. Roll croissant dough out in a circle and cut into 8 slices, place chocolate chips on each slice and shape it like a croissant
2. Whisk egg white with water and brush with egg mixture
3. Bake at 350 F for 15 minutes, remove and serve

VIETNAMESE COOKIES

Serves: *8*

Prep Time: *10* Minutes

Cook Time: *10* Minutes

Total Time: *20* Minutes

INGREDIENTS

- 8 oz. white chocolate chips
- 1 tablespoon shortening
- ½ cup butter
- ½ tsp salt
- 2 cups flour
- 1 cup sugar
- 1 tsp vanilla
- 1 egg
- 1 tsp baking powder

DIRECTIONS

1. Melt half of the white chocolate chips with a tsp of shortening
2. Cream the butter and sugar in a mixing bawl
3. Mix in melted chocolate, add baking powder, salt and mix again
4. Stir in the other half of the white chocolate chips
5. Bake at 350 F for 10-12 minutes, remove and serve

LUNCH

FISH SOUP

Serves: **4**

Prep Time: **10** Minutes

Cook Time: **30** Minutes

Total Time: **40** Minutes

INGREDIENTS

- 1 tsp coriander seeds
- 7 oz. salmon fillet
- 3 onions
- handful coriander leaves
- handful mint leaves
- juice from 2 limes
- galangal
- 2 lbs. chicken stock
- ¼ lbs. rice noodles
- 2 tablespoons fish sauce
- 2 red chillies
- 2 garlic cloves
- ¾ lbs. tail-on tiger prawns

DIRECTIONS

1. In a saucepan add galangal, stock and bring to boil for 5-10 minutes
2. Cook the noodles, drain and keep warm
3. Add fish sauce, garlic, chillies and simmer for 4-5 minutes
4. Add salmon, prawns and cook for another 4-5 minutes
5. Add herbs, lime juice, onions and cook for another 4-5 minutes
6. Pour soup in bowls and serve

CHICKEN BAGUETTES

Serves: **4**

Prep Time: **20** Minutes

Cook Time: **10** Minutes

Total Time: **30** Minutes

INGREDIENTS

- 1 chicken breast
- ½ tsp golden sugar

- juice from ½ lime
- ½ small carrot
- 2 onions
- 2 cucumbers
- 1 red chili
- 1-2 tablespoons chili sauce
- 3-4 lettuce leaves
- 1 tsp live oil
- 1 tsp rice vinegar

DIRECTIONS

1. In a pan add chicken breast with oil and cook for 3-4 minutes per side
2. Mix sugar, rice vinegar, lime juice, onion, carrot and cucumber
3. Split a sandwich baguette along the top and stuff with gem leaves and shred the chicken on top
4. Add carrot mixture, chili sauce and serve

LAMB SHANKS WITH SWEET POTATOES

Serves: *4*

Prep Time: *20* Minutes

Cook Time: *180* Minutes

Total Time: *200* Minutes

INGREDIENTS

- 2 tablespoons oil
- 3 lamb shanks
- 2 onions
- 2 tablespoons chopped root ginger
- 2 garlic cloves
- 2 red chillies
- 1 tablespoons brown sugar
- 2 lemongrass stalks
- 1 L lamb stock
- 1 tablespoons tomato puree
- 3 sweet potatoes
- 2 tablespoons fish sauce
- juice 2 limes
- mint leaves and basil leaves

DIRECTIONS

1. Preheat oven to 300 F and in a casserole add oil, season the shanks, remove the lamb add onions, add ginger, garlic and chilli
2. Add sugar and stir in lemongrass, stock, puree and seasoning and bring to boil
3. Cover and cook for 1 ½ hours and then add sweet potatoes and cook for 1 hour more
4. Stir in the fish sauce, lime juice basil leaves and serve

CHICKEN SALAD

Serves: 2

Prep Time: 5 Minutes

Cook Time: 5 Minutes

Total Time: 10 Minutes

INGREDIENTS

- ¼ rice noodle
- 1 carrot
- ½ cucumber
- 1 chicken breast

- 50g radish
- ½ red onion
- mint
- 1 oz. roasted peanut

DRESSING
- 1 red chilli
- zest and juice from 1 lime
- 1 tablespoon fish sauce

DIRECTIONS

1. In a bowl add all salad ingredients and mix well
2. In another bowl add dressing ingredients and pour dressing over salad
3. Serve when ready

PEPPER SQUID

Serves: **4**
Prep Time: **10** Minutes
Cook Time: **10** Minutes
Total Time: **20** Minutes

INGREDIENTS

- 3 oz. corn flour, 3 oz. plain flour
- 2 tsp black pepper
- 1 lb. squid
- 1 onion

DIPPING SAUCE

- 1 red chilli
- ½ cucumber
- 1 red onion
- 1 onion
- rice wine vinegar
- 1 tablespoon sugar

DIRECTIONS

1. In a bowl mix all dipping sauce and set aide
2. In another bowl mix corn flour and plain flour with peppers and salt
3. In a pan heat oil, coat squid with flour mix and cook for 2-3 minutes
4. Sprinkle with pepper and also salt
5. Serve squid scattered with onion, chilli and dipping sauce

VEGGIE HOTPOT

Serves: **4**

Prep Time: **10** Minutes

Cook Time: **20** Minutes

Total Time: **30** Minutes

INGREDIENTS

- 2 tsp vegetable oil
- 2 garlic cloves
- 2 tsp soy sauce
- 2 tsp sugar
- vegetable stock
- 3 onions
- ginger
- ¼ lb. green bean3 onions
- coriander leaves
- coriander leaves
- ½ butternut squash

DIRECTIONS

1. In a saucepan heat oil add garlic, ginger and fry for 5-6 minutes

2. Add soy sauce, sugar, squash and stock
3. Cover and simmer for 10-12 minutes
4. Add green beans and cook for another 4-5 minutes
5. Stir in the onions and sprinkle with coriander

SALMON NOODLE SOUP

Serves: **4**

Prep Time: **10** Minutes

Cook Time: **30** Minutes

Total Time: **40** Minutes

INGREDIENTS

- 2.5 lbs. chicken stock
- 2 tsp curry paste
- ¼ lbs. rice noodle
- 1 pack shiitake mushroom
- ¼ lbs. baby corn
- 2 skinless salmon fillets
- juice from 2 limes
- 1 tablespoons soy sauce
- 1 pinch sugar

- coriander

DIRECTIONS

1. Pour the stock into a pan and bring to boil
2. Add the noodles, mushrooms, corn and cook for another 10 minutes
3. Add salmon, cook for another 4-5 minutes, remove and stir in the soy sauce, lime juice and sugar
4. Sprinkle over coriander and serve

SEAFOOD SALAD

Serves: *4*

Prep Time: *10* Minutes

Cook Time: *10* Minutes

Total Time: *20* Minutes

INGREDIENTS

- 1lb. seafood mix
- ¾ lb. rice noodles
- ¾ lb. pack beansprouts

- 2 carrots
- 1 bunch onions
- bunch mint and coriander

DRESSING

- 4 tablespoons wine vinegar
- 1 tsp sugar
- 1 red chilli
- 1 stick lemongrass
- 1 tsp soy sauce

DIRECTIONS

1. In a bowl put all the salad ingredients and mix well
2. In another bowl put all the dressing ingredients mix and pour over the salad
3. Serve when ready

PRAWN SUMMER ROLLS

Serves: **10**

Prep Time: **30** Minutes

Cook Time: **0** Minutes

Total Time: **30** Minutes

INGREDIENTS

- 2 garlic cloves
- 2 tablespoons fish sauce
- juice from 1 lime
- 1 red chili
- 1 tablespoon chopped ginger
- 1 tablespoon sugar

ROLLS

- ¼ lbs. rice noodle
- handful mint leaves
- 18 cooked prawns
- 2 lettuce leaves
- 1 carrot
- handful of coriander, basil and chives
- 2 oz. beansprout

DIRECTIONS

1. For sauce pour the chili, garlic, sugar and ginger in a bowl and stir in the fish sauce and lime juice and blend using a blender
2. Soak the rice noodles in a bowl for 15 minutes and drain well
3. Dip rice papers in a bowl of hot water and place it on a board and add mint leaves and prawn halves
4. Add lettuce, noodles, cucumber, carrot, herbs and beansprouts
5. Roll tightly, to serve cut the rolls in half

CARAMEL TROUT

Serves: **2**

Prep Time: **5** Minutes

Cook Time: **10** Minutes

Total Time: **15** Minutes

INGREDIENTS

- 2 oz. sugar
- 1 red chili
- piece of ginger
- juice from ½ lemon
- coriander
- steamed rice
- 1 tablespoon fish sauce
- 2 rainbow trout fillets
- 2 heads bok choy

DIRECTIONS

1. **In a pan add sugar with water**
2. **Heat slowly and add sugar, increase heat until the syrup turns dark color**
3. **Add fish sauce, chili, ginger and water**

4. Add bok choy, fish fillets and cover the pan with a lid for 4-5 minutes
5. Turn off the heat and squeeze over the lemon and scatter with chili and ginger

PRAWN SALAD

Serves: *4*

Prep Time: *10* Minutes

Cook Time: *10* Minutes

Total Time: *20* Minutes

INGREDIENTS

- ¼ lbs. rice noodles
- 2 tablespoons peanut butter
- 3 tablespoons coconut milk
- 3 tablespoons chili sauce
- 2 onions
- 1 cucumber
- ¾ lbs. beansprouts
- 2/3 lbs. cooked prawn

DIRECTIONS

1. Cook the noodles following pack indications
2. In a saucepan melt peanut butter, coconut milk, chili, onions add, water and cook for 2-3 minutes
3. Mix the noodles, beansprouts, cucumber in a serving dish
4. Top with prawns, drizzle over the peanut sauce and scatter over onions

VIETNAMESE SALAD

Serves: 2

Prep Time: 10 Minutes

Cook Time: 10 Minutes

Total Time: 20 Minutes

INGREDIENTS

- 2/4 lbs. rice noodles
- 5 onions
- handful coriander
- 1 tablespoon roasted peanuts

ASIAN CABBAGE & PRAWN SALAD

Serves: **4**

Prep Time: **10** Minutes

Cook Time: **10** Minutes

Total Time: **10** Minutes

INGREDIENTS

- ¼ lbs. pack cooked tiger prawns
- ½ cucumber
- 1 carrot

DRESSING

- 1 garlic clove
- 1 red chilli
- 1 tablespoon sugar
- juice from 2 limes

DIRECTIONS

1. In a bowl add all dressing ingredients and mix well
2. In another bowl add salad ingredients and mix well, pour dressing over salad and serve

- 9 oz. Chinese cabbage
- 2 celery sticks
- 2 carrots
- handful mint
- handful coriander
- 2/4 lbs. peeled prawn
- 3 tablespoons roasted peanut
- 6 oz. white cabbage

DRESSING
- 1 red chili
- 2 tablespoons lime juice
- 2 tablespoons fish sauce
- 1 garlic clove
- 1 tablespoon sugar
- 1 tablespoons rice vinegar

DIRECTIONS

1. In a bowl add all dressing ingredients and mix well
2. In another bowl add salad ingredients and mix well, pour dressing over salad and serve

ASIAN CHICKEN SALAD

Serves: 2
Prep Time: 10 Minutes
Cook Time: 10 Minutes
Total Time: 20 Minutes

INGREDIENTS

- 1 boneless chicken breast
- 1 tablespoon fish sauce
- zest and juice ½ lime
- 1 tsp sugar
- ¼ lbs. salad leaves
- handful coriander
- ¼ red onion
- ½ chili
- 1/3 cucumber

DIRECTIONS

1. In another bowl add salad ingredients and mix well
2. Serve when ready

CARROT, RED CABBAGE & ONION SALAD

Serves: 2

Prep Time: 10 Minutes

Cook Time: 10 Minutes

Total Time: 20 Minutes

INGREDIENTS

- 3 carrots
- ½ red cabbage
- 1 onion
- handful mint leaves
- handful coriander leaves
- handful toasted peanuts

DRESSING

- juice 2 limes
- 1 tablespoon oil
- 1 red chili
- 1 tablespoon sugar

DIRECTIONS

1. **In a bowl add all dressing ingredients and mix well**

2. **In another bowl add salad ingredients and mix well, pour dressing over salad and serve**

PINEAPPLE SALAD

Serves: **4**

Prep Time: **10** Minutes

Cook Time: **30** Minutes

Total Time: **40** Minutes

INGREDIENTS

- 1 pineapple
- ½ cucumber
- 2 oz. cashew
- ½ lbs. cherry tomatoes
- handful mint leaves
- 5 oz. beansprout
- ½ lbs. king prawn

DRESSING

- ½ red chili
- juice 2 limes

- 1 tsp fish sauce
- 1 garlic clove
- 1 tsp sugar

DIRECTIONS

1. In a bowl add all dressing ingredients and mix well
2. In another bowl add salad ingredients and mix well, pour dressing over salad and serve

NOODLE SALAD

Serves: **4**

Prep Time: **10** Minutes

Cook Time: **10** Minutes

Total Time: **20** Minutes

INGREDIENTS

- 1 pack rice noodles
- 1 pack coriander
- 1 pack hot smoked salmon
- bread roll

- ½ lbs. snap peas
- 2 tsp sesame oil
- 3 onions

DRESSING

- 2 tablespoons soy sauce
- 1 tablespoon sunflower oil
- 1 garlic clove
- 1 tablespoon honey
- 1 tablespoon lemon juice

DIRECTIONS

1. In a bowl add all dressing ingredients and mix well
2. In another bowl add salad ingredients and mix well, pour dressing over salad and serve

PRAWN NOODLE SALAD

Serves: *4*

Prep Time: *10* Minutes

Cook Time: *10* Minutes

Total Time: *20* Minutes

INGREDIENTS

- ¼ lbs. noodle
- ¼ lbs. baby spinach
- 3 oz. cooked prawn
- ¼ lbs. snap pea
- 1 carrot

DRESSING

- 1 red chili
- 1 tsp fish sauce
- 1 tablespoon mint
- 2 tablespoons rice vinegar
- 1 tsp sugar

DIRECTIONS

1. In a bowl add all dressing ingredients and mix well
2. In another bowl add salad ingredients and mix well, pour dressing over salad and serve

ASIAN NOODLE & TURKEY SOUP

Serves: 4
Prep Time: 10 Minutes
Cook Time: 10 Minutes
Total Time: 20 Minutes

INGREDIENTS

- 1 lbs. turkey
- 1 cinnamon stick
- 2 cloves garlic
- ¼ lbs. beansprouts
- bunch coriander
- 3 onions
- 1 red chili
- 2/4 lbs. rice noodles
- 2 tablespoons fish sauce
- 2 limes
- 1 lb. roast turkey
- ¼ lbs. roast turkey
- 1 star anise

DIRECTIONS

1. In another bowl add salad ingredients and mix well
2. Serve when ready

TOFU & CASHEW STIR-FRY

Serves: **4**

Prep Time: **10** Minutes

Cook Time: **10** Minutes

Total Time: **20** Minutes

INGREDIENTS

- 1 tablespoons vegetable oil
- 3 garlic cloves
- 1 red chili
- 1 bunch onions
- 5 oz. soya bean
- 1 head pak choi
- 1 broccoli
- 2 packs marinated tofu
- 1 tablespoon hoisin sauce
- 1 tablespoon soy sauce

- 1 oz. cashew nuts

DIRECTIONS

1. In a wok heat oil over medium heat
2. Add broccoli and fry for 4-5 minutes, add water, chili and cook for another 2-3 minutes
3. Add onions, soya beans, pak choi and tofu
4. Fry for 2-3 minutes, add hoisin, soy, nuts and serve

DINNER

LEMONGRASS CHICKEN

Serves: **4**

Prep Time: **10** Minutes

Cook Time: **20** Minutes

Total Time: **30** Minutes

INGREDIENTS

- 2 tablespoons fish sauce
- 1 tablespoon curry powder
- ½ tsp salt
- 2 tablespoons sugar
- 2 lemongrass stalks
- 1 shallot
- 1 lbs. boneless skinless chicken breast
- 2 tablespoons water
- 2 tablespoons oil
- 2 chilies
- 1 scallion
- 2 garlic cloves

DIRECTIONS

1. In a bowl mix garlic, curry powder, salt, fish sauce and sugar
2. Add chicken meat to coat
3. In a skillet add sugar, water and cook on high heat, remove from heat and stir in the remaining water and move to a bowl
4. In a wok add oil over medium heat, add lemongrass, shallot, chilies and add chicken and caramel and stir-fry until chicken is cooked, serve with rice

BEAN CURD SHIK WITH SHRIMP

Serves: 3
Prep Time: 10 Minutes
Cook Time: 30 Minutes
Total Time: 40 Minutes

INGREDIENTS

- 1 lb. raw shrimp
- 2 dashes
- 2 tsp oil
- ¼ tsp sugar
- 1 egg white

- 1 stalk scallion
- 1 clove garlic
- ¼ tsp salt

DIRECTIONS

1. Rinse and devein the shrimp and dry it
2. In a food processor add shrimp, garlic, ginger and white pepper and blend until smooth
3. Transfer the mixture to a bowl
4. Beat the egg white and combine with the mixture
5. Add scallion to the mixture and divide into portions
6. Dry bean curd skin and put the shrimp paste in the middle of the bean curd and roll it
7. Heat up a wok and fry until golden brown, remove and serve

CHICKEN CURRY

Serves: 4

Prep Time: 10 Minutes

Cook Time: 30 Minutes

Total Time: 40 Minutes

INGREDIENTS

- 2 tablespoons oil
- 1 tsp sugar
- 2 oz. shallot
- 1 lb. skinless chicken thighs
- 1 can 14.5 oz. chicken broth
- ½ cup coconut milk
- 3 oz. carrots
- 5 oz. potatoes
- 1 tsp fish sauce
- 2 tablespoons curry powder
- 2 lemongrass white parts

DIRECTIONS

1. In a pot add oil over medium heat
2. Sauté the shallot until soft and add chicken
3. Stir the chicken and add lemongrass, carrots, potatoes, curry powder and stir to combine
4. Add coconut milk, chicken broth and turn heat to low
5. Cover and simmer for 20 minutes
6. Add sugar, fish sauce and mix well

SUMMER ROLLS

Serves: **4**

Prep Time: **10** Minutes

Cook Time: **10** Minutes

Total Time: **20** Minutes

INGREDIENTS

- 4 oz. rice noodles
- 4 oz. peeled shrimp
- 2 leaves fresh lettuce
- 2 oz. carrot peeled

HOISIN-PEANUT SAUCE

- 3 tablespoons hoisin sauce
- sugar
- 1 tsp roasted peanuts
- 1 tablespoon peanut sauce
- 3 tsp apple cider vinegar
- ¼ cup water

DIRECTIONS

1. In a pot add water and bring to boil, add rice noodles and boil for 4-5 minutes, drain and rise and set aside

2. Mix all ingredients for the Hoisin-Peanut sauce together in a bowl and whisk it well, transfer to a dip bowl and garnish with peanuts
3. In another pot, boil water and cook shrimp, divide in 4 portions when ready
4. Assemble the summer rolls and serve

CRAB WITH CHILI

Serves: **4**

Prep Time: **10** Minutes

Cook Time: **30** Minutes

Total Time: **40** Minutes

INGREDIENTS

- 4 lbs. crabs
- 1 red chili
- ¼ cup tooth herb
- 2 tablespoons sugar
- 1 clove garlic
- 1 onion
- ¼ cup rice paddy herb

- 1 egg
- 1 tablespoon tamarind juice
- 2 tablespoons oyster sauce
- 1 tablespoon sesame oil

DIRECTIONS

1. Place the crab on a chopping board and cut into from the crab's body, turn the crab over and pull out the long grey "fingers"
2. Cut the crab in half lengthwise through the head and remove the claws and legs
3. Heat oil in a wok over medium heat and add fry the crab pieces for 2-3 minutes
4. Mix together with egg, oyster sauce, mustard, sugar, sesame oil
5. In another wok add garlic, oil, onion and chili, cook for 2-3 minutes
6. Add tamarind and egg mixture to the wok and bring to boil
7. Add crab pieces and herb and toss for 5-6 minutes with the sauce, remove and serve

CRAB NOODLES

Serves: **4**

Prep Time: **20** Minutes

Cook Time: **10** Minutes

Total Time: **30** Minutes

INGREDIENTS

- 8 oz. mung bean
- 1 dungeness crab
- ½ small carrot
- fried shallot crisp

FISH SAUCE DRESSING

- ½ cup fish sauce
- 5 oz. palm sugar
- cornstarch mixture
- 1 tablespoon chili sauce
- 2 tablespoons lime juice
- ¼ cup water
- 1 stalk lemongrass
- 4 lime leaves

DIRECTIONS

1. Bring the water to boil and cook mung bean until tender and transfer the noodles in the pan, drain and chill
2. In a bowl mix all herbs together
3. Prepare the fish sauce dressing by mixing all ingredients in a sauce pan and simmer on low heat, add corn starch mixture
4. Stir in the garlic chili sauce and lime juice and let dressing chill, assemble crab noodles and serve cold

GARLIC NOODLES

Serves: 4

Prep Time: 10 Minutes

Cook Time: 10 Minutes

Total Time: 20 Minutes

INGREDIENTS

- 20 oz. noodles
- 1 tablespoon grated parmesan cheese

DRESSING

- 1 stick butter

- 1 tablespoon minced garlic
- 1 tablespoon fish sauce
- 1 tablespoon sugar
- 1 tablespoon seasoning sauce
- 1 tablespoon oyster sauce

DIRECTIONS

1. In a pot boil water, add noodles into the water and cook until al dente, when ready transfer the noodles out
2. In a pan add garlic sauce over medium heat, add butter, garlic, and sauté
3. Add seasoning into the pan and stir well
4. Toss all the noodles with garlic sauce and serve

LEMONGRASS BEEF SKEWERS

Serves: **20**

Prep Time: **15** Minutes

Cook Time: **15** Minutes

Total Time: **30** Minutes

INGREDIENTS

- 1,5 LBS. SIRLOIN STEAK
- 20 wooden skewers

MARINADE

- ½ cup lemongrass
- 1 tablespoon sesame oil
- ½ tsp salt
- 2 tablespoons garlic
- 2 tablespoons soy sauce
- ½ tsp black pepper
- 2 tablespoons fish sauce
- 2 tablespoons sugar
- ½ cup minced shallot

DIRECTIONS

1. In a bowl add all marinade ingredients and mix well
2. Add marinade to the meat and mix well, let it marinade for at least 1 hour
3. Insert the meat through the wooden skewers
4. Grill the meat for 3-4 minutes per side
5. Garnish with sautéed scallion and serve

SRIRACHA GRILLED SHRIMP

Serves: **4**

Prep Time: **20** Minutes

Cook Time: **10** Minutes

Total Time: **30** Minutes

INGREDIENTS

- 1 lb. tiger prawn
- 4 skewers
- oil

MARINADE

- 2 tablespoons fish sauce
- 1 lemongrass
- 1 tablespoon sugar
- 1 tsp sriracha
- 1 clove garlic

DIRECTIONS

1. In a bowl add all the ingredients for the marinade
2. Stir to combine well with the shrimp and marinade for 15-20 minutes

3. Brush the surface of the shrimp with oil and grill on both sides until they are cooked
4. Serve with dipping sauce

POK POK WINGS

Serves: **4**

Prep Time: **10** Minutes

Cook Time: **20** Minutes

Total Time: **30** Minutes

INGREDIENTS

- ¼ cup fish sauce
- ½ cup cornstarch
- 8 cloves garlic
- 1 tablespoon cilantro
- 1 tablespoon mint
- ¼ cup sugar
- 1 lbs. chicken wings
- 1 tablespoons vegetable oil

DIRECTIONS

1. In a bowl whisk the fish sauce, garlic and sugar, add the chicken wings and toss to coat, refrigerate for 2-3 hours
2. In a skillet heat oil, add garlic and cook for 3-4 minutes
3. In a pot heat oil over medium heat and add cornstarch, wings and turn to coat, fry the wings until golden for 8-10 minutes
4. In a saucepan simmer the marinade over high heat for 4-5 minutes, top with cilantro, garlic and serve

BANH MI WIH LEMONGRASS PORK

Serves: **4**

Prep Time: **10** Minutes

Cook Time: **30** Minutes

Total Time: **40** Minutes

INGREDIENTS

- 2 lbs. boneless pork
- ½ bunch cilantro leaves
- 4 jalapeno chilies

- picked carrots
- mayonnaise
- 4 8-inch baguette rolls

LEMONGRASS PORK MARINADE

- ½ cup lemongrass
- 2 tablespoons fish sauce
- 2 cloves garlic
- 1 tablespoon sesame oil
- 1 tablespoon cooking oil
- 1 tablespoon black pepper
- 4 shallots
- 1 tablespoon soy sauce
- ½ cup sugar

DIRECTIONS

1. In a bowl mix all marinade ingredients, add pork slices and marinade for 2-3 hours or overnight
2. Preheat grill and cook the meat 5-6 minutes per side
3. Remove pork from grill and assemble baguettes, add Jalapeno chilies, mayonnaise, pork, carrots, cilantro leaves and serve

LEMONGRASS SHRIMP

Serves: **2**

Prep Time: **10** Minutes

Cook Time: **10** Minutes

Total Time: **20** Minutes

INGREDIENTS

- 1 tablespoon oil
- 1 onion
- 1 tablespoon lemongrass
- 2 chilies
- 10 oz. shelled shrimp
- 1 tablespoon hoisin sauce
- 1 tsp fish sauce
- ½ cup water
- 1 stalk scallion

DIRECTIONS

1. In a wok heat oil over medium heat, add lemongrass, onion, chilies and shrimp
2. Stir until the shrimp is cooked, add hoisin sauce, water, fish sauce and stir well

3. Add scallion into the wok, remove and serve with rice

SPRING ROLLS

Serves: **4**

Prep Time: **10** Minutes

Cook Time: **20** Minutes

Total Time: **30** Minutes

INGREDIENTS

- 5 oz. pork
- 1 egg
- 2 oz. shrimp
- salt & pepper
- shredded carrots
- 1 oz. crab meat
- 1 tsp fish sauce
- 1 oz. mung bean noodles
- 1 clove garlic
- 1 shallot
- 2 dashed black pepper

DIRECTIONS

1. In a bowl mix the all ingredients together
2. To roll the cha gio place a piece of rice paper on a towel and place a tablespoon of filling on the rice paper
3. Heat oil over medium heat in a wok and fry them until golden brown
4. Remove and serve with lettuce leaf

CARAMEL SHRIMP

Serves: **4**

Prep Time: **10** Minutes

Cook Time: **20** Minutes

Total Time: **30** Minutes

INGREDIENTS

- 1 lb. shrimp
- 1 tablespoon fish sauce
- ¼ tsp black pepper
- 1 shallot
- 1 bunches of scallion

CARAMEL SAUCE

- 2 soup spoons of cooking oil
- 1 tablespoon sugar

DIRECTIONS

1. In a pan add oil and sugar over medium heat, once the sugar takes a caramel color, set aside
2. In a skillet heat oil add the prawn and sauté for 2-3 minutes
3. Add caramel sauce until the shrimp sucks the the sauce, serve when ready

GRILLED SHRIMP WITH GREEN PAPAYA

Serves: *4*

Prep Time: *10* Minutes

Cook Time: *30* Minutes

Total Time: *40* Minutes

INGREDIENTS

- 1 green papaya
- 1 green mango

- ½ jicama
- 1 carrot
- ½ cup chopped peanuts
- fresh mint
- fresh cilantro
- 1 thai chile
- shrimp

DRESSING

- ½ tsp garlic paste
- 1 tablespoon sugar
- ½ cup lime juice
- ½ cup thai fish sauce
- 1 tablespoon mint
- 1 tablespoon cilantro stems

DIRECTIONS

1. In a bowl mix papaya, carrots, mango, jicama and herbs
2. In another bowl whisk all the ingredients of the dressing
3. Place the shrimp on skewers and season with salt, grill for 2-3 minutes per side
4. Pour the dressing over the salad and serve

CARAMEL CHICKEN

Serves: **2**

Prep Time: **10** Minutes

Cook Time: **10** Minutes

Total Time: **20** Minutes

INGREDIENTS

- 1 lb. chicken thighs
- 1 tablespoon oil
- 2 cloves garlic
- ½ jalapeno

MARINADE

- 1 tablespoon sugar
- 1 tablespoon fish sauce

CARAMEL SAUCE

- 1 tablespoon fish sauce
- 2 tablespoons water
- ½ tablespoon sugar
- 2 tsp rice vinegar

DIRECTIONS

1. In a bowl mix all marinade ingredients and add chicken and mix all in and set aside for 10-15 minutes
2. In another bowl mix all the caramel sauce ingredients and set aside
3. In a skillet heat oil over medium heat and fry the chicken until brown, remove the chicken when ready
4. Add garlic in the skillet, add the chicken into the pan and caramel sauce
5. Let it simmer for a couple of minutes, add jalapeno and cook for 1-2 minutes, when ready remove and serve

SUGAR CANE SHRIMP

Serves: **4**

Prep Time: **10** Minutes

Cook Time: **30** Minutes

Total Time: **40** Minutes

INGREDIENTS

- 1 lb. raw shrimp
- 1 egg white
- ¼ tsp sugar

- 2 dashed fish sauce
- 1 dash white pepper
- 1 tsp lard
- 2 cloves garlic

DIRECTIONS

1. In a food processor add shrimp, pepper, garlic, oil and blend until smooth, transfer the mixture to a bowl
2. In a bowl beat the egg, mix the shrimp with the mixture and beaten egg, refrigerate
3. Heat up a wok and fry the shrimp until golden brown

CHICKEN WINGS

Serves: *4*

Prep Time: *10* Minutes

Cook Time: *30* Minutes

Total Time: *40* Minutes

INGREDIENTS

- 1-2 lbs. chicken wings

- 8 cloves garlic
- ¼ cup fish sauce
- ½ cup sugar
- 2 dashes black pepper
- 1 tablespoon peanuts
- 1 tablespoon cilantro

DIRECTIONS

1. In a bowl, fish sauce, garlic, sugar, black pepper, stir to mix well
2. Add the marinade to the chicken wings, combine well with the marinade, marinade for 2-3 hours
3. Preheat oven to 350 F, bake for 25-30 minutes until golden brown, top with cilantro and serve

LEMONGRASS WINGS

Serves: **4**

Prep Time: **20** Minutes

Cook Time: **10** Minutes

Total Time: **30** Minutes

INGREDIENTS

- 2 tablespoons lemongrass
- 2 stalks lemongrass
- 1 lb. small chicken wings
- 2 tablespoon fish sauce
- 4 garlic cloves
- 1 tablespoon honey
- ½ tsp black pepper

DIRECTIONS

1. Take the chicken wings and transfer to a Ziploc bag and add all the ingredients inside
2. Combine everything well and add fish sauce and lemongrass mixture and let marinate in the fridge overnight
3. Fire up the grill until and grill the winds until golden brown, remove and serve

GRILLED CHICKEN BANH MI

Serves: **6**

Prep Time: **10** Minutes

Cook Time: **50** Minutes

Total Time: **60** Minutes

INGREDIENTS

- 1-pound boneless chicken thighs
- 1 tablespoon lime juice
- 1 tablespoon canola oil
- ½ tsp sugar
- ½ tsp salt
- 1 tsp black pepper

DIRECTIONS

1. In a bowl add sugar, pepper, fish sauce, lime juice, salt
2. Add oil and chicken and coat well, cover with plastic and marinade
3. Preheat the grill and cook the chicken for 5-10 minutes and turn several times, until clear juices
4. Remove and cool before serving

DESSERT

SINH TO – FRUIT SHAKE

Serves: **1**

Prep Time: **5** Minutes

Cook Time: **5** Minutes

Total Time: **10** Minutes

INGREDIENTS

- ½ banana
- 3 tablespoons condensed milk
- ice
- 1 tsp sugar

DIRECTIONS

1. **In a blender add all ingredients and blend until smooth**
2. **Pour in a glass and serve**

VIETNAMESE EGG ROLLS

Serves: **20**

Prep Time: **10** Minutes

Cook Time: **10** Minutes

Total Time: **20** Minutes

INGREDIENTS

- 2 lbs. pork
- 1 tablespoon pepper
- 1 tablespoon cornstarch
- 1 tablespoon garlic powder
- 2 eggs
- 1 lb. ground turkey
- 20 oz. cabbage
- 20 oz. carrot
- 4 oz. onion
- 2 bundles bean thread
- 2 tablespoons sugar
- 5 tablespoons fish sauce

DIRECTIONS

1. Chop the noodles into one inch strips and set aside

2. In a blender, blend pork and turkey together, add pepper, garlic powder, cornstarch, sugar, add beaten eggs, fish sauce and blend well
3. Add carrot, cabbage, onion and blend again
4. In a Dutch oven add 2-3 oz. of filling, roll it from the bottom up and tuck the point underneath the filing
5. Fry until golden brown, remove and serve

COFFE CRÈME FLAN

Serves: **6**

Prep Time: **10** Minutes

Cook Time: **10** Minutes

Total Time: **20** Minutes

INGREDIENTS

- ½ lbs. condensed milk
- 3 egg yolk
- 2 tsp vanilla extract
- 1 lbs. milk
- 4 eggs

DIRECTIONS

1. Melt sugar in 4-5 spoons of water, mix with coffee
2. Mix well all ingredients, pour into bowl with caramel
3. Bake for 30-45 minutes at 275 F
4. Remove, let it cool and serve

STICKY RICE WITH COCONUT

Serves: *4*
Prep Time: *10*   Minutes
Cook Time: *30*   Minutes
Total Time: *40*   Minutes

INGREDIENTS

- 1 cup rice
- sesame seeds
- sugar
- ½ cup black beans
- roasted peanuts
- coconut
- salt

DIRECTIONS

1. Rinse soaked beans and cook until soft
2. Rinse soaked rice, mix with boiled beans and put on steamer
3. Add water, salt and cook on medium heat
4. Cook for about 15-20 minutes, serve with coconut, peanuts or sesame seeds

FRIEND SPRING ROLLS

Serves: **6**

Prep Time: **10** Minutes

Cook Time: **20** Minutes

Total Time: **30** Minutes

INGREDIENTS

- 20 oz. shrimps
- 1 carrot
- mushrooms
- handful white cabbage

- 1 oz. rice noodles
- 2 shallots
- 1 clove garlic
- 1 egg
- oil
- mint
- salt & pepper

DIRECTIONS

1. Mix all ingredients except oil, mint pepper and salt
2. Put the mix on a piece of rice paper and wrap
3. Heat up oil in wok and cook for 10-12 minutes
4. Remove and serve with herbs or dipping sauce

PAPAYA MIX

Serves: 4
Prep Time: 10 Minutes
Cook Time: 10 Minutes
Total Time: 20 Minutes

INGREDIENTS

- 1 green papaya
- 1 carrot
- 1-inch fresh ginger
- 1 tablespoon sugar
- 1 tablespoon vinegar
- water
- ½ tablespoon fish sauce

DIRECTIONS

1. Mix sugar with vinegar, ginger and water
2. Mix well and stir into mix of papaya and carrot
3. Serve with different Vietnamese dishes

SUGAR CANE JUICE

Serves: *4*
Prep Time: *10* Minutes
Cook Time: *30* Minutes
Total Time: *40* Minutes

INGREDIENTS

- 1 sugar cane stick
- 3 limes
- ice cubes

DIRECTIONS

1. Peel sugar cane, squeeze it and add limes
2. Serve with ice

VIETNAMESE BROWNIE

Serves: 8
Prep Time: 10 Minutes
Cook Time: 20 Minutes
Total Time: 30 Minutes

INGREDIENTS

- 10 tablespoons butter
- 1 cup sugar
- ½ tsp salt

- ¾ cup cocoa powder
- 2 tablespoons coffee
- 1 tsp vanilla extract
- 2 eggs
- ½ flour

FROSTING

- 8 tablespoons butter
- salt
- 1 tsp vanilla extract
- 2 cups sugar
- 2 tablespoons condensed milk

DIRECTIONS

1. In a bowl mix butter, sugar, coffee, cacao and salt, transfer to a skillet
2. Heat over barely simmering water, until mixture is melted
3. Stir in vanilla, eggs and flour, beat vigorously
4. Spread evenly in a pan, bake for 25 minutes
5. For the frosting beat butter with mixer, add vanilla and salt
6. Beat in powdered sugar and condensed milk until smooth
7. Spread on cooled brownies

VIETNAMESE COFFE FLAN

Serves: 8

Prep Time: 20 Minutes

Cook Time: 60 Minutes

Total Time: 70 Minutes

INGREDIENTS

- ¾ cup sugar
- 14-ounce can condensed milk
- 3 cups milk
- 4 eggs
- 4 tsp instant coffee
- 1 tsp vanilla
- ¼ tsp salt

DIRECTIONS

1. **Preheat oven to 350 F**
2. **In a saucepan cook sugar over medium heat, pour mixture into a baking dish**
3. **Blend the remaining ingredients until smooth, pour custard, then transfer dish to a roasting pan place place it in the oven**

4. Bake for 60-70 minutes, remove and let it cool

VIETNAMESE ICED COFFE

Serves: **1**

Prep Time: **5** Minutes

Cook Time: **5** Minutes

Total Time: **10** Minutes

INGREDIENTS

- 12 ICE CUBS
- ½ cup condensed milk
- 2 cups brewed coffee
- 3 ground coffee

DIRECTIONS

1. In a blender add all ingredients and blend until smooth
2. Pour in a glass and serve

VIETNAMESE AVOCADO SMOOTHIE

Serves: **1**

Prep Time: **5** Minutes

Cook Time: **5** Minutes

Total Time: **10** Minutes

INGREDIENTS

- 1 avocado
- ¼ cup condensed milk
- ½ cup milk
- 1 cup ice cubes

DIRECTIONS

1. **In a blender add all ingredients and blend until smooth**
2. **Pour in a glass and serve**

VIETNAMESE EGG SODA

Serves: **1**

Prep Time: **5** Minutes

Cook Time: **5** Minutes

Total Time: **10** Minutes

INGREDIENTS

- 2 tablespoons condensed milk
- 1cup soda
- ice
- 1 egg yolk

DIRECTIONS

1. **In a blender add all ingredients and blend until smooth**
2. **Pour in a glass and serve**

VIETNAMESE COFFEE POPS

Serves: *1*

Prep Time: *5* Minutes

Cook Time: *5* Minutes

Total Time: *10* Minutes

INGREDIENTS

- 2 cups brewed coffee
- 1 pinch ground cinnamon
- ½ cup condensed milk

DIRECTIONS

1. In a blender add all ingredients and blend until smooth
2. Pour in a glass and serve and add wooden sticks in them
3. Refrigerate, remove and serve

VIETNAMESE EGG COFFEE

Serves: **1**

Prep Time: **5** Minutes

Cook Time: **5** Minutes

Total Time: **10** Minutes

INGREDIENTS

- 1 cup coffee
- 2 egg yolks
- 1 tablespoon heavy cream
- 1 tsp vanilla extract

DIRECTIONS

1. **In a blender add all ingredients and blend until smooth**
2. **Pour in a glass and serve**

VIETNAMESE YOGURT

Serves: *1*

Prep Time: *5* Minutes

Cook Time: *5* Minutes

Total Time: *10* Minutes

INGREDIENTS

- 12 oz. condensed milk
- 1 cup hot water
- 1 cup milk
- 1 cup yogurt

DIRECTIONS

1. In a bowl mix condensed milk with water
2. In another bowl whisk yogurt with mix until smooth
3. Pour condensed milk into yogurt mixture and mix well
4. Pour into individual containers and refrigerate

VIETNAMESE COFFEE FRAPPE

Serves: **1**

Prep Time: **5** Minutes

Cook Time: **5** Minutes

Total Time: **10** Minutes

INGREDIENTS

- 2 cups coffee
- 2 tablespoons condensed milk
- 1 cup ice cues
- 5 cups water
- ½ cup brewed coffee

DIRECTIONS

1. **In a blender add all ingredients and blend until smooth**
2. **Pour in a glass and serve**

COCONUT MILK COFFEE

Serves: **1**

Prep Time: **5** Minutes

Cook Time: **5** Minutes

Total Time: **10** Minutes

INGREDIENTS

- 1 tablespoon ground coffee
- 1 tablespoon boiling water
- 1 cup ice cubes
- 24 coffee creamer

DIRECTIONS

1. **In a blender add all ingredients and blend until smooth**
2. **Pour in a glass and serve**

CHERRY SMOOTHIE

Serves: **1**

Prep Time: **5** Minutes

Cook Time: **5** Minutes

Total Time: **10** Minutes

INGREDIENTS

- 2 cups frozen cherries
- 1 cup ice
- 1 cup almond milk
- 1 tsp almond extract
- ½ tsp cinnamon

DIRECTIONS

1. In a blender add all ingredients and blend until smooth
2. Pour in a glass and serve

VIETNAMESE GRANITA

Serves: *1*

Prep Time: *5* Minutes

Cook Time: *5* Minutes

Total Time: *10* Minutes

INGREDIENTS

- 2 cups coffee
- 1 tablespoon Frangelico
- ½ cup condensed milk
- ½ cup sugar

DIRECTIONS

1. **In a blender add all ingredients and blend until smooth**
2. **Pour in a glass and serve**

VIETNAMESE GREEN SMOOTHIE

Serves: **1**

Prep Time: **5** Minutes

Cook Time: **5** Minutes

Total Time: **10** Minutes

INGREDIENTS

- 10-ounces vanilla almond milk
- ½ cup frozen raspberries
- ½ tsp Saigon
- 1 tablespoon honey
- 1 cup frozen mango
- ½ cup chopped kale
- salt

DIRECTIONS

1. **In a blender add all ingredients and blend until smooth**
2. **Pour in a glass and serve**

THANK YOU FOR READING THIS BOOK!

Made in United States
Troutdale, OR
01/01/2024